AMERICAN PRESIDENTS

FRANKLIN D. ROOSEVELT

INDIA JAMES

NORWOOD HOUSE PRESS

Cataloging-in-Publication Data

Names: James, India.
Title: Franklin D. Roosevelt / India James.
Description: Buffalo, NY : Norwood House Press, 2027. | Series: American presidents | Includes glossary and index.
Identifiers: ISBN 9781978579811 (pbk.) | ISBN 9781978579828 (library bound) | ISBN 9781978579835 (ebook)
Subjects: LCSH: Roosevelt, Franklin D. (Franklin Delano), 1882-1945--Juvenile literature. | Presidents--United States--Biography--Juvenile literature. | Legislators--United States--Biography--Juvenile literature.
Classification: LCC E807.J36 2027 | DDC 973.917092--dc23

Published in 2027 by
Norwood House Press
2544 Clinton Street
Buffalo, NY 14224

Designer: Rhea Magaro
Editor: Kim Thompson

Photo credits: Cover, p. 1 The White House; pp. 4, 5, 7, 9-11, 13-16, 19, 21 Library of Congress; p. 8 NARA;

Printed in the United States of America

CPSIA compliance information: Batch #CSNHP27: For further information contact Norwood House Press at 1-800-237-9932.

TABLE OF CONTENTS

Early Years

Franklin Delano Roosevelt was born on January 30, 1882, in Hyde Park, New York. He lived in this house with his mother and father. His half-brother was 28 years older.

The Roosevelt family was rich. Franklin's parents did not have to work very often. They spent a lot of time with young Franklin. They took vacations in Europe every year. They visited their cabin near Eastport, Maine.

When Franklin was young, **tutors** helped him learn. He did not go to school until he was 14 years old. When he was 18, he went to Harvard University.

Building a Career

Franklin graduated from college in 1904. Then, he went to Columbia Law School. He learned how to be a **lawyer**.

Franklin married Eleanor Roosevelt in 1905.

The two were distant cousins.

Franklin became a popular **politician**. He was elected to the New York state **legislature** in 1910. He was elected governor of New York in 1928 and 1930.

At the time, many people suffered from **polio**. It was a dangerous and contagious disease. Franklin caught it in 1921. He got better, but he was **paralyzed** from the waist down. He used a wheelchair to move around.

Presidency

In 1933, Franklin became the 32nd president of the United States. There had already been a President Roosevelt. Franklin's cousin Theodore Roosevelt was the 26th U.S. president. For this reason, Franklin came to be known by his initials: F.D.R.

Many people were poor when Franklin was president. America was in the **Great Depression**. There were not enough jobs for everyone.

Franklin started programs that helped people get money, food, and jobs. One was the Civilian Conservation Corps (CCC). It paid men to plant trees and build parks and roads. Franklin gave a name to all his programs. He called them the New Deal.

People were thankful that Franklin had helped them during hard times. They elected him president again in 1936 and 1940.

World War II began in Europe in 1939. Franklin tried to keep the U.S. out of the fighting. In 1941, he agreed to enter the war. He worked with the leaders of other countries to plan and organize.

Legacy

Franklin was elected president for a fourth time in 1944. He started his **term** but died on April 12, 1945. Americans remember him as a caring leader. They remember how he helped people and led the country during war.

Glossary

Great Depression (grate di-PRESH-uhn): a time from 1929 to 1939 when many people did not have a lot of money

lawyer (LAW-yur): a person whose job is to understand the law and fight for people in court

legislature (LEJ-is-lay-chur): a group of people who have the power to make or change laws for a state or country

paralyzed (PAR-uh-lized): unable to move

polio (POH-lee-oh): an infectious disease that attacks the brain and spinal cord, that can cause paralysis, and that is now prevented by a vaccine; short for *poliomyelitis*

politician (pah-li-TISH-uhn): a person elected or chosen to hold a government office

term (turm): a definite or set period of time; American presidents are elected to a term that lasts four years

tutors (TOO-turz): teachers who give private lessons

Thinking Questions

1. What disease left Franklin paralyzed?
2. Why did people call Franklin F.D.R.?
3. What was the New Deal?
4. What did Franklin do during World War II?
5. How many times was Franklin elected president?

Index

About the Author

India James writes about science, technology, math, and history for young readers. She loves learning new things while writing books. India lives in Ohio with her family.